D0500660

Sources for Library Materials in FY09   2.6%
Albany County Public Library

■ Cash Gifts
■ Public Money   45.0%   52.5%
☐ Donated Items

MUDDY AS A DUCK PUDDLE
AND OTHER AMERICAN SIMILES

by **Laurie Lawlor**
illustrated by **Ethan Long**

Holiday House / New York

For Keira Marie Beaudoin
L. L.

For Kevin Moore, my old, old friend
E. L.

What is a simile?

Pronounced **sim**-uh-lee, this figure of speech compares two different things, actions, descriptions, or feelings. Most similes are introduced by *as* or *like*.

"As pretty as a new-laid egg."

A simile can create a fresh, surprising description. A simile can even make us laugh when it sets up the opposite of an expected meaning.

"As welcome as a polecat at a picnic."

Text copyright © 2010 by Laurie Lawlor
Illustrations copyright © 2010 by Ethan Long
All Rights Reserved
HOLIDAY HOUSE is registered in the U.S. Patent
and Trademark Office.
Printed and Bound in October 2009 in Johor Bahru,
Johor, Malaysia, at Tien Wah Press.
The text typeface is Billy.
The art for this book was created digitally using
Photoshop with lasso and paint bucket.
www.holidayhouse.com
First Edition
1 3 5 7 9 10 8 6 4 2

Library of Congress Cataloging-in-Publication Data
Lawlor, Laurie.
Muddy as a duck puddle and other American similes /
by Laurie Lawlor ; [illustrated by Ethan Long].
p. cm.
ISBN 978-0-8234-2229-6 (hardcover)
1. English language—Parts of speech. I. Long, Ethan ill. II. Title.
PE1199.L39 2010
425'.5—dc22
2009029944

Alike as two peas.

Busy as a stump-tailed cow
in fly-time.

Crooked as a barrel of snakes.

Dark as
a pocket.

Easy as shinnying up
a thorn tree
with an armload of eels.

Fine as frog hair.

Gritty as fish eggs rolled in sand.

Happy as a clam
at high water.

Independent
as a hog on ice.

Keen as a briar.

Lazy as a hound that leans
against the fence to bark.

Muddy as a duck puddle.

Nimble
as a weasel.

Ornery as a skunk.

Pretty as a
new-laid egg.

Quick as a minnow
can swim a dipper.

Red as a gobbler's snout
in spring.

Safe as a possum
in a pie.

Tight as a new boot.

Ugly as a mud fence dabbed over with toad frogs.

Vain as a peafowl
with two tails.

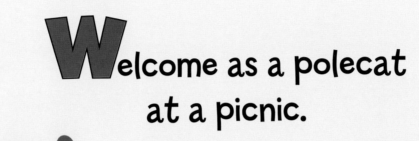

Welcome as a polecat
at a picnic.

X-eyed as a staggering, buckeyed calf.

Yellow as
a flitter tree that grows
beside a honey pond.

Zany as a chigger
chased around a stump.

AUTHOR'S NOTE

"I told him stories that were enough to set the Mississippi afire."
—James K. Paulding
Westward Ho! (1832)

American folk expressions used in this alphabet book are more precisely known as "proverbial comparisons." This seems like a mouthful to describe what is essentially shorthand: ready-made phrases that provide colorful, to-the-point comparisons.

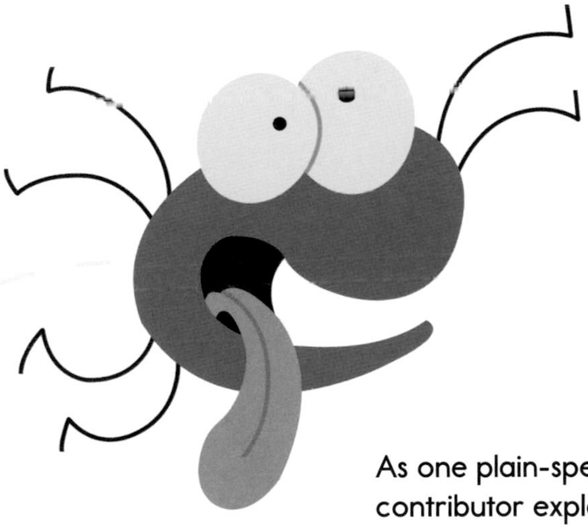

As one plain-speaking contributor explained, "You don't have to fish around for no decorated language to make the meaning clear."

Americans from all walks of life and from all parts of the country have contributed to this collection. And yet most of the expressions that appear here have uncertain origins.

They were passed down from generation to generation by word-of-mouth before they were ever recorded in print. Some came across the Atlantic Ocean with the first immigrants from the British Isles. Other expressions were influenced by Native American languages. Many may have origins in languages of Europe, Central America, South America, Africa, and Asia. Wherever restless Americans have settled, they have taken their expressions with them—adapting old sayings, discovering new ones.

The incorporation of these phrases into American speech was especially significant after America ceased to be a colony of England. As settlers pushed west, south, and north more than two hundred years ago, their speech became uniquely American. Many of the expressions reflect the boisterous tall talk and exaggeration that produced legendary characters such as Mike Fink, Paul Bunyan, and Pecos Bill. American English embodied a new spirit that historian Thomas Pyles called "self-confident, daring, pushful, uncouth, obsessed with the notions of greatness and strength . . . quite unlike anything that had been known before."

Alike as two peas.
Wisconsin

Almost identical. This farm-inspired phrase is one used commonly in Wisconsin and elsewhere throughout the Midwest. The origin is uncertain.

Busy as a stump-tailed cow in fly-time.
Ozarks

Occupied to the point of being frantic. Flies during warm summer months plague cattle, whose only defense is their flapping tails. Picturesque comparisons such as this one are a striking feature of the speech of the hillmen who live in the Ozarks.

Crooked as a barrel of snakes.
Ozarks

Very crooked; sometimes dishonest. One of many everyday expressions collected by Arkansas newspaperman Vance Arnold on a fishing trip near Noel, Missouri, in the early 1930s. He also noted "crooked as a dog's hind leg."

Dark as a pocket.
Wisconsin

This was one of many earthy expressions collected by Mrs. Clarice Moon of Delavan, Wisconsin.

Easy as shinnying up a thorn tree with an armload of eels.
Ozarks

A difficult, hazardous job. Along the same theme, a Missouri congressman reportedly described a tricky political maneuver: "It's a good deal like climbin' a greased pole with two baskets of eggs."

Fine as frog hair.
Indiana

In good health. Other variations: "fine as frog hair quartered" and "fine as frog hair split in the middle." Frogs don't have hair, so where did this expression come from? Nobody seems to know for certain. One explanation might be that the phrase implies an exaggeration. Instead of just replying, "I'm fine," the speaker responds, "I'm fine as frog hair." In other words, "I'm *very* fine." This phrase was jotted down by a researcher during the summer of 1938, while he was collecting folklore in ten counties in southern Indiana.

Gritty as fish eggs rolled in sand.
American West

A cowboy's description of a brave person. This phrase reflects a collection of cowmen's vocabulary put together by writer Ramon F. Adams during thirty years of travel across the West, from Texas to North Dakota and from Nebraska to California, "to help preserve this lingo for posterity."

Happy as a clam at high water.
Virginia

Safe and secure. Protected by the high tide, clams are concealed from their enemies that prowl the beaches and tidewater areas of Virginia. This phrase was collected by tireless B. W. Green in 1899, who scoured the state for folk sayings and peculiar Virginia expressions, many of which may have been transported from the seaports of sixteenth-century Devonshire and southwestern England.

Independent as a hog on ice.
Wisconsin

Anyone who refuses badly needed advice or help—perhaps to his or her own detriment. The phrase's origin appears to be somewhat mysterious. There are many different explanations for this phrase. How can a hog be "independent" on ice? Some writers believe that the *hog* referred to is not a farm animal but a marker used in the Scottish game of curling. In this game, flat stones are slid along ice. Another explanation might be that a hog does not go on ice until after it's butchered. Yet another possibility is that long ago many farmers in remote settlements did not pen their hogs. Instead, they turned their hogs out into the forests to find food for themselves (the origin of another phrase: "root, hog, or die.") When butchering time came around, perhaps the clever hogs tried to run away across frozen streams in order to make their capture more difficult.

Jittery as a long-tailed cat in a room full of rocking chairs.
Wisconsin

Very nervous. A Wisconsin expression that might describe the nervous cat's exit out the door: "faster than a cat lappin' chain lightning."

Keen as a briar.
Ozarks

Sharp as a thorny shrub. A common expression in the Ozarks that has as its opposite: "dull as a frow." This refers to a tool used long ago to split wooden shingles and clapboards. An unsatisfactory knife is described as "so dull you could ride to mill on it."

Lazy as a hound that leans against the fence to bark.
Tennessee

Very lazy. Variation on this comparison comes from Virginia: "as lazy as Hall's dog that lent against the fence to bark." Who was Hall? His name has passed on through the years but not his identity.

Muddy as a duck puddle.
Virginia

Perhaps the variation on this might be "ducky as a mud puddle."

Nimble as a weasel.
Ozarks

Reportedly said by a farmer in Garland County, Arkansas, while describing a wiry, little gambler.

Ornery as a skunk.
Mississippi

Indicates a terrible temper. "Ornery" is a southern expression derived from "ordinary." The New World translation indicates not only "mean" but "stubborn," "poor," "inferior," and "bad."

Pretty as a new-laid egg.
Ozarks

Often describes an attractive girl. Beauty is in the eye of the beholder. To a cowboy, the phrase is "pretty as a red heifer in a flower garden."

Quick as a minnow can swim a dipper.
Ozarks

Illustrates incredible speed. One-room schoolhouses often used buckets with long-handled dippers for students to scoop up drinking water. A small, wriggling fish did not need much time to swim across a dipper and cause a practical joke sensation.

Red as a gobbler's snout in spring.
Ozarks

In the wilderness, early settlers were very aware of the habits of flocks of wild turkeys, which were often hunted for food. In early spring the male turkey, or tom, begins its courtship display to attract a mate. The tom's caruncle, a flap of skin on the forehead, turns red and flops down over the beak. When this happens, the concealed beak (or snout) looks red.

Safe as a possum in a pie.
Ozarks

This Ozark expression seems to fall into the same category as "pleased as a skunk in a churn" and "calm as a hog on ice." The meanings aren't always what they seem. Most likely the possum is hiding inside the pie, enjoying a feast. The possum is often described as a clever survivor. "If a cat has nine lives," goes an old North Carolina saying, "a possum has nineteen." "To possum" means "to pretend or fake." When about to be captured, the hunted opossum flops on the ground with its eyes closed and muscles limp, and acts as if it's dead. Early American hunters noted this behavior of the wily animal that only springs back to life when it's doused with water. The saying is thought to have been circulating in the United States for at least two hundred years.

Tight as a new boot.
Ozarks

Describes a particularly stingy person. An Ozark variation along the same theme: "tight as beeswax."

Ugly as a mud fence dabbed over with toad frogs.
Tennessee

Describes an extremely homely individual.

Vain as a peafowl with two tails.
Ozarks

Proud backwoods beauty. Phrase is usually used to describe a particularly haughty woman.

Welcome as a polecat at a picnic.
American West

Cowboy expression for a person who has worn out his or her welcome. Such an individual might also be described as "his cinch is gettin' frayed." (His saddle has been on his horse too long.) Other variations include "welcome as a rattler in a dog town" and "pop'lar as a tax collector." Such a person is one to be avoided. "Folks go 'round 'im like he was a swamp."

X-eyed as a staggering, buckeyed calf.
Ozarks

X-eyed, signifying "cross-eyed," appears in the *Dictionary of American Slang* published in 1934 by Maurice H. Weseen of Lincoln, Nebraska. Weseen admits, "Slang is by nature free and vivacious, often to the point of irreverence. Much of it is grotesque. To a considerable extent it represents defiance." In the Ozarks, a calf who has nibbled on buckeyes is an animal that has been poisoned and is not long for this world.

Yellow as a flitter tree that grows beside a honey pond.
Ozarks

A fruitful region. Jack Short of Galena, Missouri, was said to have used this phrase in describing his congressional district: a place of milk and honey where it was easy to make a living. A flitter is a pancake. "Flat as a flitter" is another common Ozark expression.

Zany as a chigger chased around a stump.
Ozarks

A chigger is a tiny, jumping bug with a nasty bite. A variation on this: "There's so many chiggers here that a tick-bite is a kind of enjoyment." "Zany" dates back to the commedia dell'arte in Italy of the sixteenth to eighteenth centuries. In these theatrical productions, the *zanni* (Italian) was a buffoon who made fun of the stock characters. The English altered the spelling to "zany" to mean anybody who was a bumbler or fool.

BIBLIOGRAPHY

Adams, Ramon F. *Western Words: A Dictionary of the American West.* Norman, OK: University of Oklahoma Press, 1968.

Brewster, Paul G. "Folk Sayings from Indiana." *American Speech* 14 (1939): 261-68.

———"More Indiana Sayings." *American Speech* 16 (1941-42): 21-25.

Funk, Charles E. *A Hog on Ice and Other Curious Expressions.* NY: Harper, 1948.

———*Heavens to Betsy! And Other Curious Sayings.* NY: Perennial Library, 1986.

Gard, Robert Edward, and L. Sorden. *Wisconsin Lore.* NY: Duell, Sloan & Pearce, 1962.

Green, B. W. *Word Book of Virginia Folk-Speech.* Richmond, VA: William Ellis Jones Book Publishers, 1899.

Hardie, Margaret. "Proverbs and Proverbial Expressions Current in the United States East of the Missouri and North of the Ohio Rivers." *American Speech* 4 (1929): 461-72.

Hendrickson, Robert. *Whistling Dixie Dictionary of Southern Expressions.* Vol. I. NY: Facts on File, 1993.

———*Mountain Range Dictionary of Expressions from Appalachia to Ozarks.* Vol. IV. NY: Facts on File, 1997.

Morris, William and Mary. *Morris Dictionary of Word and Phase Origins.* NY: Harper & Row, 1977.

Randolph, Vance, and George P. Wilson. *Down in the Holler: A Gallery of Ozark Folk Speech.* Norman, OK: University of Oklahoma Press, 1953.

Weseen, Maurice H. *Dictionary of American Slang.* NY: Thomas Y. Crowell and Co., 1934.

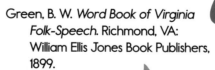